Permission To Thrive

Shawn Pearson

This book is based on facts and events that have made a difference in the author's life. The life lived has a lot of messages to pass on to the next person in their lives and in their community.

The message in this book is one of living through failures as well as accomplishments.

Farabee Publishing
Chandler, Arizona, 85224
www.Farabeepublishing.com

Printed in the United States of America

Book Cover designed by David Mor

ISBN: 979-8-88796-768-4

Dedication

Being called to a position of leadership is an honor and also the task, especially if you are a woman. I recognize that I have been called to a position of leadership that requires me to share my personal experiences with developing into a woman of virtue. This is not something that has come easy because for much of my life, I neither understood the definition of virtue nor believed that I had the capacity to achieve it.

I have been called to a work of breaking the cycles and break the chains to create women of virtue. This means I am going to be a nontraditional leader in the sense that the way God is using me may contradict much of the tradition that we have learned in the modern church. I am not the kind of leader who will sit quietly in disagreement when I hear someone teaching scripture incorrectly. Incorrect teaching almost cost me my life, literally. Because I had incorrect and incomplete teaching about the Word of God, I was left vulnerable. I found myself in a position of hopelessness. I was hopeless to the point that I wrote letters of apology to my family members for the way that I had failed them and then attempted suicide.

You see, I spent my whole life trying to measure up, trying to be loved by others. I have been an overachieving child in hopes that it would change my relationships with my father and my mother. I later became an overachieving girlfriend who would do whatever my boyfriend asked me to do, just for the sake of feeling loved and accepted by him.

Later, I grew into the overachieving, yet inexperienced wife. You would think that surviving the suicide attempt would have been something that brought me joy. But instead, it made me feel like even more of a failure.

I believed that I could not even achieve this successfully. The fact that I felt hopeless enough to take such desperate actions would not seem so surprising for someone who didn't "know the Lord".

At the age of 19, I accepted Christ as my Lord and Savior, believing that this singular act of surrender would transform my life and move me from the place of misery after the death of my mother. I was only 18 when she passed from cancer, at the tender age of 47.

So, at the tender age of 47, I have made the decision to publish this book in honor of my mother, Anna Marie Williams, who passed away with so many unfulfilled dreams. My prayer is that this book will be filled with lessons that will help other beautiful, outgoing, intelligent yet broken women to break the cycles, break the chains and become women of virtue.

Instructions

If you are reading this book, I'd like you to follow these simple instructions:

1) Commit to finishing the book.
2) Use the Personal Reflection pages to answer these questions:
    a. What do I see in my life that is familiar?
    b. How does this hold me back?
    c. What steps can I take to begin to change it?
3) Seek help or support where/when you recognize that you need it. This won't be easy, but it will be worth it.
4) Send me a Facebook message to share your experiences as

you read – Shawn M. Pearson, Journey Coach

Lesson #1-We Have a Choice to Make

"We will never be forced into greatness. When God gives us instructions, we must CHOOSE to follow them."

There are so many times in my life where I wanted to be better than I was on my journey to be righteous. A lot of times the secret disappointments in secret Shane get me from reaching out to others in the Church body that could have possibly lifted and encouraged me. Nevertheless, I would struggle through whatever the situation or circumstance wearing a mask. When I was too weak to wear the masks anymore, I fainted. In my fainting, I attempted to take my own life. Even though man didn't see my pain, God did.

That experience was the beginning of my journey with God on a much deeper level. I thought the worst was over, but I was in for a surprise. The persecution and suffering should not have been a surprise because the Bible talks about it in several places. The sad part is that it was a surprise for me, even as a believer, because I wasn't being taught the whole truth and nothing but the truth. Nor was I studying the Word of god for myself. I don't say that as an indictment on the church. I don't speak it as an indictment on my pastors or leaders who did attempt to teach me all that they knew. The point that I want to make is that studying the word for myself became so paramount to my own literal survival.

We can't trust our salvation, our thriving, our prosperity to what is said to us from the pulpit, in a Bible study lesson or by well-meaning people. **We must learn who God is for ourselves**. Our relationship with him has to be as personal and as intimate as our relationships with our children, our spouses, or any other people that we love and dedicate our lives to.

Sharing my testimony about my attempted suicide had become easy to do after repeating it over a series of years. However, confronting all of the dysfunction that still exist and in my life despite being saved was a very different story. Being saved didn't take away my belief system that have been instilled in me from childhood through early adulthood and even my 30s. In fact, there were so many knowledge gaps about the word of God that I have begun to except some of the things that I had endured as just part of the program from God's plan of salvation.

In ignorance, it was easy for me to except that the rest of my family might never be saved and that the only time I would have just been with them would be during this earthly life. It was easy to except living in poverty because, I could look around me and many other Christians were living in par birdie too, so it was not unusual nor was it unacceptable to me.

I could accept working a full-time job and doing consulting on the side just to make ends meet at home to provide for my children because I look at life from a rational perspective. I could except that teaching Sunday school in a small church was the limit to the ministry that God placed in me because I had come from poverty and didn't have much to offer anyone else.

I could accept all of the generational curses of mental health issues, alcoholism, sexual abuse, physical abuse, poverty, absent fathers, promiscuous girls, struggle, strife... The list could go on. Instead, one day I got fired up.

Making a decision to take my journey to virtuous was not an easy one. The first thing that I had to do was believe that I could actually be better than what I saw in the mirror. Every day for the first 34 years of my life I believed that I wasn't worthy of a man who was truly manly.

When I say "manly," I'm referring to a man who is a provider and a protector and most of all a lover of the Lord Jesus Christ.

I always settled for a male that had at least one of the essential characteristics. But I could never seem to attract one who put God before himself and was a good example for me and all the other people in their sphere of influence.

In this state of compromise, I was okay with the man who drank excessively, or who had extra women on the side as long as I was his main squeeze. I was really good at making excuses for their behavior or being in denial about it when I was confronted with the truth.

My solution to coping with their shortcomings was to assimilate and become like them in order to feel accepted and continue to receive their imperfect definition of love.

By age 30, I was fully convinced that I should be alone because my picker was broken. The way that I picked a mate was completely flawed. I chose the abuser, the addict, the Playboy, the chauvinist. I decided that I wouldn't be involved with any male except for my son who was approaching his teenaged years.

I can remember being challenged by a particular gentleman who wanted to take me on a date. He told me one day over lunch that he was going to make me love him. I took it upon myself to spend the next eight months punishing this one man for all the sins of every man who had ever hurt me.

I did it all at his expense. Or at least I thought it was all of his expense. I was his trophy and he was what we would call my sugar daddy. He often spent money on me and took me about the town to show me off to his friends. He was at least 16 years my senior but it didn't matter. I was determined to prove that I was in control of my own emotions. I had no true reverence for the things that he did for me or for any kindness that he attempted to show me. My mission was to prove that I could be just as hard and emotionless as the men whom I had trusted with my heart.

By the end of this eight-month saga, this gentleman told me that he had invested approximately $5500 in our relationship and I should at least consider a modified sexual arrangement and provide him with sex as a Christmas present. Being the young angry woman that I was, I shared some very unpleasant sentiments with this so-called gentleman and told him that he would need to add a few zeros before his offer could even be considered.

Needless to say, that ended the drama that was my sugar daddy experience. I spent the next few months avoiding him and trying to go places that were as far away from him as possible. Somewhere in the whole twisted relationship he had decided that he truly cared for me. By the way, I forgot to mention that this man had been legally separated, not divorced, for a few years from his wife and had children that were very near to my age.

The sinful nature and the justified my actions by saying I'm not the one who is married. I was legally divorced from my ex-husband and this man had been legally separated for some years.

I don't have to tell you that this was adultery. I only had to be honest with myself. Some years later, I acknowledged the mess that I had created and forgave myself for my shameful behavior that I had excused because of my bitterness. My divorce was soon final and I could legitimately "date" again. Let me just say, like Paul said, "all things may be lawful, but not prudent."

Since I still wasn't ready to begin my journey to virtuous, I began to date another older man. Something in me believed that dating an older man would provide some safety and security that I had lacked and longed for all of my childhood and adult life. Wow, this gentleman was indeed a lover of God.

He was also a lover of work. There were very few times that we arranged a date that didn't have to be canceled because something came up at the office or at one of his businesses.

This man of God treated me like a queen, but I was very impatient. I wanted all of his time, at least all of his time that he wasn't spending on the job. I had no life to speak of, other than going to work every day and providing for my three children.

There was not much social activity even though I was in the prime of my life and totally capable of making friends if I had desire to do so. All I craved was the company of a man, because I felt so inadequate from the rejection and failed relationships from my past. I was determined to find a man who would make me his pride and joy and would put me before his friends, before his addictions, before the other women, before his job, before everything and everyone.

If I have been honest with myself, I would have admitted that I even wanted this man to put me before God.

This relationship was very short-lived because I didn't feel like I was the priority. The loneliness in his absence made me very vulnerable. But even in my vulnerability, I would pretend to be that virtuous woman that I should be.

I pretended that I was saving myself for this man that should someday be my husband. The reason that I say I was pretending it's because my heart was not truly chaste. If he is willing to have intercourse with me I will gladly given myself outside of marriage just to prove to him that I "loved" him.

When I look back on that season of knowing this gentleman, I believe that God was attempting to demonstrate to me that I had value beyond what I carried physically. He was trying to show me that there was a man who would respect who I was and what I had to offer, even if I wasn't offering sex.

If only I have been smarter. I ended the relationship with this gentleman because he could not give me all the time and attention that I wanted. Although he was quite comfortable financially, I had never desired to be married to or attached to a man simply for his paycheck.

I was too proud of a woman who was making my own money. Although I had some struggles from time to time, I was proud to say that no one was paying my bills except me. Even if I had needed help, I was too proud to ask for it. My motto was never let them see you sweat.

I never had the courage to just tell him that I wanted more of his time more attention. I simply decreased my calls and decreased my visits. He was wise enough to know that things had changed and he was not the type to pursue me if it was not welcomed. Shortly after we stopped dating, we happen to attend the same event in the community.

Each of us had another date on her arm. I was extremely jealous and regretful for not being honest with him before. That was the last time that I saw him for any extended period of time.

Personal Reflections

Lesson # 2- Your Mindset Matters

"What you believe about yourself is more powerful than what anyone else believes about you. You don't have to accept the myth that you are a product of your environment. What you really are, is a product of our Creator."

I can hear Carol King playing in the background, and my mother staring me in the face. It's 3 o'clock in the morning on a school night. She's got tears in her eyes, as she stares at me so seriously, asking the question, "who…are…you?."

As a child, my first instinct, is to say my name, of course. What other answer could there be? But Momma had something else in mind. She was trying to instill something in me that I was too young to comprehend. The correct answer to her question was, "I am a survivor." Momma was trying to prepare me for life. She was trying to prepare me to never be a quitter, regardless of my circumstances.

My mother was certainly no saint. Her imperfections were extremely impactful on my life and even more so for my brothers. But even in that, this one lesson of survival I do remember. This seed of survival that was planted in my soul as a little girl was truly a belief that helped me endure many hardships and tragedies- including her early death when I was 18 and pregnant.

I carried this belief that I was a survivor into every part of my life. No matter what I encountered, I believed that it couldn't break me. Not abuse, not poverty, not rejection! These things couldn't stop me.

I was a survivor. But as I grew older, I recognized that while I always survived, I was not yet thriving. I was 30 before I even recognized the difference between surviving and thriving.

As a survivor, I was merely existing. I was always in some sort of struggle.

I expected struggle. I expected hard times. I expected to just get by using my wit and intellect to narrowly escape demise. The thrill that I called success was just staying a step ahead of utter ruin. I was a chaos junky. I was a struggle junky. I identified with the struggle and I was good at it: so good that others in the struggle admired me for "making it."

This "making it" was simply not being on welfare, living in the projects on Section 8. Since I had three children, that's what statistics determined to be my fate. However, the survivor in me worked a job and did small jobs on the side to make ends meet.

I started my first business at 25 to bring in extra income because my ex-husband's addiction interfered with him keeping a steady job. Franklin Enterprises was the name of the business. We provided residential and commercial cleaning services. During the week, I worked in a hospital. On the weekends, I cleaned homes and office spaces. Once again, I was the over-achieving survivor.

For more than 10 years, I contemplated the notion of thriving. I was so familiar with simple survival. The thought of having more than enough, and abundance, was counter intuitive for me. I had never been trained not to struggle. What would that even look like? How would I navigate the waters of being free of financial stress?

How could I adjust to no worrying which bill would have to be rotated? The fact of the matter was that Momma taught me what she knew, and I needed it for a season in my life. But that season was over. It had been over for years. I was afraid to let go of the familiar training to step into a new place that God needed me to be in for His purpose.

It was time for me to step into a new place. In order to get there, I needed a new guide with new instructions. I needed to be trained by someone who understood a thriving lifestyle.

I needed to be trained by mentors who understood God's commandments for the purpose of wealth.

He gives us the ability to get wealth in order to establish His covenant here on the Earth. I was being called to a new place so that God could use me to establish His promises for His people, right now.

So, how do I retrain my thoughts? How could I, as Pastor Walter H. Walker says, pre-play my future instead of replaying my past? For 30+ years, I was Shawn the Survivor. Now I have to become something new, because the survivor never has enough to share and bring others out of bondage. A survivor barely has enough for themselves. I began to search the Word of God, again and again and again.

I was looking for what God said about me. Who does God say that I am? I had to find thoughts and beliefs to replace those that had taken root in my soul. Those thoughts that told me I wasn't good enough, pretty enough, smart enough, wealthy enough, just ENOUGH. I had to erase the voices of men who discouraged me and so-called friends who discounted me because of my circumstances. I had to denounce the words of church folk who had spoken negative things about me because I didn't measure up according to tradition.

I had to see myself building my own dream. I had to draw out my own road map and blueprint. I had to humble myself and seek help from people who demonstrated that they had the answers to my questions about the Word of God and about business.

How did I do this?

I looked for their fruit. I sought counsel from Godly women whose husband's spoke highly of them, like in Proverbs 31. I didn't just look for someone in church with a title or position. I sought counsel from businessmen who had demonstrated their ability to gain wealth through running businesses.

I didn't just look for someone in business, but rather someone who did business with integrity.

In ministry, I look for pastors and leaders who were working outside of their own church walls; those leaders who truly followed the command to "go into all the world and preach the gospel." I looked for what these people were producing in their own lives and in the lives of others.

What else did I do?

I began to look in the mirror daily and say what God says about me. He says that I am fearfully and wonderfully made, in His image and His likeness. There's a lot more that the Word of God says about who we are, as His children. Then I finally started to believe that I was more than a survivor. I had graduated from Momma's school of hard knocks.

Personal Reflections

21

Lesson # 3-Discipline is Key to Your Journey

"Without discipline, all the little shiny things and beautiful distractions can delay and derail your journey."

Out of the frying pan into the fire! The next season for me was one filled with new experiences. I had decided that I would just focus on me and the children. My routine was pretty limited. I would go to work, come home, feed the children, watch television, and do homework.

Recreation consisted of visits to the park and visits with family but there were no friends around. I didn't realize it at the time, but I had isolated myself from the rest of the world maybe attempting to insulate myself from any more pain that might come from trusting others.

In the midst of my time of just babysitting me, my daughters convinced me to enter a beauty pageant. Being the tomboy that I had been as a teenager and even young adult, participation in a pageant was far too feminine for me. I did not like to wear make-up. I certainly did not like prancing around in evening gowns and swimsuits.

The thought of being paraded around in front of an audience was very unattractive. However, the thought of sharing a bonding moment with my daughters was exciting. I wanted my girls to have experiences that I never had as a child. I wanted them to feel beautiful and to be courageous and outspoken in their beauty.

I know I'm biased, but my girls were and still are very talented. My youngest was very outspoken, even as a small child. She was articulate and intelligent. She had beautiful dark hair and a very charming smile with deep dark glistening eyes that pierced the soul.

My oldest girl was much more soft-spoken. She was very charming and unassuming Lee funny. Her milk chocolate skin was always so soft and pretty and her hair was soft and cottony. Both the girls were very loving and warm spirited. I just knew that participating in the pageant would give the world a chance to see all the beauty that I had enjoyed in them for so many years.

So, I committed to these regular rehearsals and spending money that we really didn't have and even wearing make- up. I know my son must have been driven crazy by all of the girly activities that were going on around the house and preparation for this pageant. We were rehearsing poems and practicing choreography and singing all around the house.

When the day of the pageant came, I remember looking at the other contestants that were in my age category. There were a couple of strange birds, but there are also some very beautiful and elegant looking women of all shapes and sizes. Some of the women had athletic body others of the women were very voluptuous.

I am the other hand, was what I considered to be a plain Jane. I was a little more around on the bottom but very lacking in the breast area. I figured that I could compensate for my lacking physique with my charm and intellect in other categories. I had no real desire ambition to win, I only wanted to be engaged in an activity that would show my darters how much I appreciated their beauty.

As the hours rolled by each stage of the competition created more and more anxiety for me. Watching the other women strut and perform and carry themselves in such a sophisticated way in their gowns was very intimidating to me. I had always seen myself as the girl who looked like her brothers, only with more hair. Since I was in the Mothers category, our group was the last group to perform and display our talents and attire.

It was very exciting to see my daughters singing and being excited to display their talents. But when it was my turn, I have butterflies beyond belief.

I can remember very distinctly completing my oral presentation. The judge asked me if I were a bicycle which part of the bicycle what I be?. I responded to him that if I were a bicycle I would be the front wheel so that I could go wherever I was told to go. He responded by asking me, "if you are front wheel then who would be the handlebars?"

I responded by saying, "God would be the handlebars, so that he could guide me in every direction that I might take". I could tell by his raised eyebrow that he was intrigued by my answer. I move down the line to the next judge for my next question. I felt pretty confident that I had at least nailed the oral presentation. I was always good at saying the right things, even if I couldn't do the right things.

When it came time for us to display our talent, I watched a young woman in my age group performs fabulously to very upbeat songs. I remember thinking that I wished I had only been as agile and as limber as she had been. I wished I could dance half as good as she did for her performance. Her performance was followed by a young woman who was very strange.

This young lady provided quite a bit of humor for all of the contestants in the pageant. From time to time when I got a little heavy hearted, it was nice to see her to remind myself to keep my motions light and just try to have fun with this whole thing. She performed a monologue that was as bizarre as her multicolored hair and multicolored sash and very vibrant make up.

I was so lost in her attire that I could hardly pay attention to the word she spoke. Up next was a strikingly beautiful older woman. I could tell she was much more mature and sophisticated than me. This way of her hips and the gloss of her lips told the story before she even spoke.

She had beautiful silky hair. She was tall and very well proportioned. She was definitely bigger than a model but big in all the right places. As she walked to the stage I remembered admiring her beauty and the need to myself that someday I will be viewed as being pretty just like she is. She began to recite the poem by Maya Angelo, phenomenal woman.

The words flowed methodically from her lips and I was entranced just as I'm sure the judges were. And suddenly there was a pause. She had forgotten the words. As she paused to try and remember the words, she stood very graciously with a smile on her face, as if the pause was naturally part of the performance.

They she continued and completed the poem to the end. The applause from the crowd ring out and snapped me out of my trance. I remember thinking that I would rather climb underneath the stage and pretend like I wasn't a participant in the pageant anymore. There was no sense in attempting to follow her beauty or her sophistication on the stage with my attempt to compete.

When the mistresses ceremony called my name for me to approach the stage, she walked away with the microphone. I was left to perform without a microphone. I was torn for a moment because I felt it might be a blessing in disguise in case I forgot the words to my poem.

So, I sat down in my chair with my big hat that covered one eye and my leopard spotted rap that I had fashioned as a dress and began to recite a poem that I had authored called a woman redeemed.

I stood from the chair, just as I had rehearsed, and walked to the edge of the stage attempting to make eye contact with guests in the audience. I felt so vulnerable at that moment. A woman redeemed was a heartfelt expression of all that I had desired from everyman that I had ever loved.

Just as I walked to the left of the stage to make eye contact with the judges as they had trained us to do in our rehearsals, one of the judges tapped his ear. He was tapping his ear to suggest that they could not hear me as I recited my poem. Just as we made eye contact I recited the line of the poem that said, "give me love respect and trust, and quality time is a must."

I went on to finish the poem and ended perfectly as I was seated back in the chair with my hat tipped over my right eye and my legs crossed and my hands on my hips. In that moment I truly felt like a woman redeemed. I had said all the things I needed to say in the open to a crowd of strangers. I have said all of these things courageously and even with a bit of sass and my voice.

The crowd shared their applause and I left the stage went to the back room to get dressed.

Personal Reflections

29

Lesson # 4 Failures is Your Boot Camp Experience

"Instead of looking at the multiple business ventures as failures, I learned to use them as learning tools to perfect my performance. Don't allow disappointment to make you doubt the dream. Use it as fuel to climb the ladder toward success."

"Many are the afflictions of the righteous, but God is a deliverer out of them all."

Man, oh man! This scripture was made real in my life on my journey to becoming a successful mother, wife, minister, and entrepreneur. I was challenged by obstacles in every area of my life. It seemed that I was not realizing success anywhere, and it was very discouraging.

For years, I made it a practice to put more energy into the places where I felt I was achieving the best. If that was work, I did overtime. If that was marriage, then I invested more time in dating and such with matching outfits and all the mushy things young couples did in the 90s. If it was parenting, I became Betty Crocker and made cookies and served as Softball Mom.

Sadly, this practice only meant that I was avoiding the other areas of my life. Of course, this made things even worse. I didn't know how to pause and examine my failings. I didn't know how to ask for feedback from the people around me, including my loved ones, to learn from their observations. I had a mental picture of what my life should look like. If I didn't meet that expectation, I considered myself a failure.

My life had no balance. Better yet, my life had no harmony. Expecting balance between three children, a spouse and a career was unrealistic.

There was never time to give equal attention to everything going on in my world. I had a season of being beaten into submission by the rapid fire of failure all around me.

It seemed as if everything I had touched was falling apart. The most important thing that was falling apart… was me.

My health took a dive. All the racing and running and rescuing that was a regular part of my routine was summarily arrested. Superwoman was on lock-down. No work, no play, no rescue. I could barely sit upright on the sofa or go to the restroom without assistance. The most torturous part of it all was that I had no end date in sight. I couldn't even plan my return to superhero status. I was forced to just sit and think.

This season of solitude was agonizing at first. All I could think about was how I was letting everyone down. I wasn't there for them. I couldn't handle everyone's business and build their dreams for them. All I could do is rehearse all my own failures. What a drag.

I didn't drink alcohol either, so my pity parties were pretty boring. Day after day rehearsing all the things I did wrong. I replayed in my mind how much of a disappointment I had been. To make matters worse, this wasn't the first time I had been sick like this.

It was more like the 9th or 10th time. The first time it happened after moving to Arizona, my car got repossessed for non-payment. I couldn't get released from the doctor to return to work, so I had no means of paying the bills.

I had no idea how I would come out of this jam. In the past, I could pull in some consulting work and make extra money. This time, I felt helpless. I felt stuck. Even though I had family around who was willing to help me, I felt so alone and responsible for fixing myself so I could get back to work.

Being stuck on the couch to replay all my failures turned from punishment to revelation when I finally discovered a pattern.

In between pain medication and sleeping, I was taking time to write down my ideas for how to make money.

I had to do something to get myself out of this whole. After all, the superhero always found a way of escape when they were trapped in the movies.

As I wrote down and reflected on all my ideas, I recognized that each new idea really wasn't new at all. I was replaying old steps, but each time I made it a little further along on the journey. I realized that my first business went for a few months and the next for a year.

The third lasted for 2 years and the fourth made it to 5 years. What could I learn from these reflections? Here I was in the first year of yet another business, and I was flat on my back. Being the analytical person that I am, I started to examine how each business ended.

I looked first, of course, at what I did that hurt the businesses. Then I look at what did I not know that hindered each business. I considered what additional help would have made the difference. I even reflected on what I could do differently if I were to launch each business again. After a while, it didn't feel like punishment anymore to be sequestered to my couch.

My husband could come home and I would actually be pleasant instead of whiny.

These weeks of reflection turned into research. I researched my personal habits. I examined my professional habits. I had to take a good hard look at my areas of weakness and make a commitment to find the help I needed to bring about change. For me, this meant asking for help. I meant saying no to some things and focusing on just a few projects at a time. This even meant finding partners and mentors to help build my dream, rather than jumping ship to go build someone else's dream.

After some failed partnerships and collaborations, I found a right fit. But those others didn't feel like failure anymore. I call them my pilot projects.

All these mini projects helped me to improve in my areas of weakness and they made me wiser for this journey. I learned to pick myself back up each time I fell. I learned to reflect on why or how I fell. Then I committed to persevering on this journey.

When I am tempted to stop, I think about how hard it would have been for me if my mentors and coaches quit without ever getting a chance to help me. Then I think about who might be waiting to hear my story and be coached or mentored by me.

Thinking about people like me, like you, keeps me motivated to learn from my mistakes and keep sharing my stories.

Personal Reflections

Lesson # 5- Stay Focused on Your Destination

"On your journey, you will encounter many people who don't believe in your dream. However, be sure to stay in communication with God to reaffirm His declaration. Your encounters with rejection can cause you to lose focus if you don't keep your eyes on God's promise".

You will keep in perfect peace those whose minds are steadfast, because they trust in you.

Isaiah 26:3

Of all the things that I would consider to be barriers to my success, the rejection endured by friends, family and loved ones was by far the most difficult to overcome. The lack of financial resources was a challenge. But it was not unfamiliar to me. I was raised in poverty and I learned to survive in poverty before the concept of thriving was even a reality to me. The biggest enemy to my success was REJECTION.

This familiar foe is something that haunted me from childhood. I can remember **desiring** the attention of my mother or my father. I can remember the loss of my older brother, who was like a father to me. I can remember feeling unaccepted by family members because of other adult drama that I didn't understand within the dynamics of our family dysfunction.

I can remember having a crush on little boys, who had a crush on other little girls. I can remember not feeling welcomed at my new schools when our neighborhood school was shut down.

All of these memories from childhood translated into "I'm not good enough" in my heart. I never said it out loud or even realized it when I was young. I simply went into my young adult life being an over – achiever who felt I had to earn love and acceptance.

I was the "A" student. I was the sacrificial girlfriend who told the lie to keep my friends out of trouble.

I was the promiscuous teenaged girl who gave sex to prove my love. Later, I became the overly submissive wife who made excuses for the affairs and verbal abuse. I was the wife who hid the physical abuse out of shame because I subconsciously felt that I had done something to deserve it.

"If I could just be a better…." Whatever title I used to complete this sentence didn't matter. My reality was that I would do whatever I thought was necessary to avoid being rejected.

This mentality was detrimental to every great promise that waited for me beyond my wilderness. As long as I defined myself by this wrong interpretation of my identity, I was vulnerable to making foolish mistakes in my quest for validation from people. I needed acceptance. I needed credentials. I needed approval. I needed the support of the people around me before I would embrace anything good in my life.

This behavior translated into every area of my life- marriage, parenting, family relationships, my worship, and my business. I had to change my mentality and then change my focus.

Changing my focus began with focusing on who and what God says I am. I had to focus on the promises and the declarations made about me by the One who made me. It was a literal reprogramming of my thinking. This reprogramming required a daily commitment to visiting my identity, my purpose, and my dreams.

I had to replace the negative thoughts, words and actions with declarations that provided hope and motivation toward my dreams. I had to write it down. I had to do research about other people who had been successful in the areas where I desired to go. I researched these people for the purpose of learning from their journey, not to mimic them.

I am a firm believer that we don't all have to endure something in order to prove that it is painful. I can learn from someone else's mistakes if they are willing to share their journey.

This is why I am so excited to share my journey with you. I want your journey to be easier than mine. What are you longing to achieve? What do you have to overcome first?

Write down your dream. Don't just do this one time. Write it down daily. Speak it as often as you think it. Begin to pre-play your future in your mind and with your mouth. Speak it until you can feel it deep down in your soul. Speak it until you experience excitement at the thought of being close to achieving it. Focus on it.

Now… discover what God has said about you at the same time. Know who you are and what you are capable of achieving. There will be people around you who will try to get you to believe what they believe. They will try to get you to buy in to their limitations. Don't do it. Resist the temptation to fit in or be accepted by adapting to someone else's opinion of you.

You are GREAT! You have the ability to be healthy, happy, and prosperous in every area of your life. You have to believe this. I am living proof that society and statistics do not define who you are. Your environment does not determine who you become. Your decisions guide you to your destination. If you focus on the lack and the challenges that you have experienced, you hold back your promise. If you focus on your greatness and your abilities that are gifts to you, you can walk into your destiny.

What are you focused on right now? Is it bringing you closer to or farther away from your destiny? Who are you hanging around? What kind of company do you keep? Are they positive people who inspire you to be better than you are? Are these people who lend a hand or offer wisdom to help you achieve your dream?

Or maybe you are hanging out with doubting folks who have no aspirations to be anything more than what they are now.

Maybe you are hanging out with people who have a victim's mentality. You know the ones who "can't" because someone else is holding them back.

They "can't" because they don't have enough, or know the right people, or live in the right neighborhood, or have the right job. They don't have the college degree so they aren't educated enough. They have too many kids, so that can't make their dreams happen.

ALL THINGS ARE POSSIBLE TO THOSE WHO BELIEVE!

We can find an excuse or we can make it or motivation. Yes, it may be hard, very hard. But hard doesn't mean impossible.

Focus on your destination and don't be derailed by the distractions. Anything or anyone who offers doubt as a response to your dream is NOT a good influence. Like I mentioned before, I had people very close to me doubt my declaration of being a Beautiful Black Billionaire.

Some were people whom I highly respected and loved. But I couldn't and can't let them stop me. I have no room in my heart or my head for their doubt. I'm too busy pressing past my own emotional luggage to see my destiny. The more I repeat my destination, the more real it becomes.

The more I focus on my destination, the harder it is to see the other mess in the background. My eyes are laser focused. My actions and my words are aligned with my destination.

Today, rejection is just a sign that I am on a right path. When I am being accepted by too many folks from too many places, I have to check myself to make sure I'm not conforming out of complacency or falling back into my old habits of seeking acceptance.

I check for the fruit that is being produced in the lives of the people who want to me around me, or who I find myself being around often. I have to make sure that the circles that I am in are still pointed toward my destination.

I have to stay focused on my identity and my destiny.

Personal Reflections

42

Lesson # 6 Know the Difference Between Tradition and Truth

"Not knowing the difference between truth and tradition can be deadly."

"Cleanliness is next to godliness."

"God helps those who help themselves."

"Money is the root of all evil. "

"Family that prays together stays together."

"If you just get married instead of shacking up God will bless it."

Logically speaking. All of these sayings that I heard and my past make sense. However, I was never able to find them in the Bible. Like many other traditions and sayings, these inaccurate beliefs could be fatal to an undeveloped soul in Christ.

I've always been very fond of family traditions. Even though we're not so close now, when I was a child I can remember our family tradition of Christmas and Thanksgiving being hosted at my grandmother's house.

I look forward to the big meal with all the home cooked dishes and special recipes from my aunts and my grandmother. I also remember tradition of a stir and frost cake for our birthdays when we were little. It took me until I was in my late teens to realize just how poor we actually were when I was young. I would imagine that a stir in frost cake was about all my mother could afford.

The word wasn't practice in my household, of the members of our family had a tradition of going to church. My mother was not a churchgoer. However, I have an aunt who would pick me up some weekends to attend church. I can remember the tradition of a new hairdo and a new dress for Easter Sunday.

I really look forward to those new outfits each year. All of the family traditions seem harmless enough. I managed to get a nice meal and a new outfit as a result of all of them. The one thing I wish I had gotten from our traditions associated with church was a right understanding about The Bible

As I mentioned before, I gave my life to the Lord at age 19. I met a wonderful woman who loved the Lord beyond anything I have ever witnessed. Her name was Brenda. But I called her sister Rainer. I met Brenda as a result of dating her son, whom I later married.

To observe Brenda's relationship with God was such a fascinating experience for me. I had never seen someone so faithful and so positive and so powerful in their walk with God. It was in Brenda's living room that I surrendered my life to Christ and made a commitment to live according to the word of God.

Little did I know that this commitment was more than just the single actor that I had taken in that living room. Making a decision to live for Christ would be a lifelong journey and pursuit of the spiritual maturity. I was so naïve. I've believed that all I needed to do was make this confession and "the end" ..."she would live happily ever after".

After giving my life to Christ I assumed that all of the heels of my childhood would disappear and the life of property that we can do it would be all gone away. After all my family members

Who attended church had nice homes, nice car, wonderful marriages, and all of the fairytale fixings. At least that was how I saw it as a little girl. Now fast forward to age 19, I had one child and my mother have been deceased for less than one year. I was desperate for a sense of belonging and a sense of being.

I thought that all I needed to do was to mimic the behaviors that I saw from the happy "churchgoers". So, when Brenda told me that I needed to get married rather than live in sin with her son, I believed it to be true and I got married.

At the time of my life, I was little baby Christian. I took what the seasoned Saints said as the gospel and I did not get into the Bible and study for myself to learn the truth. If I had I am certain that I would have not chosen to be married nor would I have chosen to allow A man who is not my husband to live in my home.

It took me 10 more years after meeting Brenda and two failed marriages to learn that I am fearfully and wonderfully made in the image of God. It didn't take me another five years to forgive myself for all of the wrong choices I made as a result of walking in darkness.

Have you ever made a decision with incomplete information? I mean a life changing mind-altering decision that you fill out have any eternal impact.

If you have, then let me reassure you that God's love covers a multitude of faults and his grace is absolutely sufficient for us.

The tradition that I have followed let me to make the decision to marry a man that I did not know well enough to be living with, much less building a family. The truth that I did not know would have delivered me from the bondage of shame and abandonment.

What are the traditions you hold that may sound good but do not align completely with scripture?

Turning point in my life that brought me from traditional into truth was the attempt to in my life.

Personal Reflections

Lesson # 7 Always Examine Yourself for Alignment

Many of the people in my circle had benefited a great deal from my lack of confidence. I spent years in the shadows helping to build the dreams of other visionaries. God had blessed me with an ability to see the road map for other people's visions, as they shared them with me.

I can't count how many times I would be having a conversation with someone else about what they wished they could achieve. It would be some organization or some program. Instantly, I could begin to visualize the blueprint for how to get them to a place of accomplishment.

For many years, I would volunteer to write business plans and grant proposals for people who were excited about their dream. But I wouldn't apply that same gift to my own dreams.

I had become an excellent silent partner and cheerleader for others. I never sought credit for anything that I was doing. It just felt good to see someone succeed or accomplish a goal to live their dream. I didn't keep track of the money they made or the success they were achieving.

It didn't matter to me, because I didn't see myself in the same category as them anyway. I was afraid to live my dream. Sure, I could talk about it. But I had a million excuses for why my dreams couldn't be achieved. I wasn't educated enough. I wasn't financially fit enough.

I was just a single mother. I didn't have the right support. I didn't have enough time. My life wasn't righteous enough. I had too much sin in my past and too much shame in my present to change my future. Until…

The burden to help heal the souls of men and women in the church became so unbearable that I would lose sleep at night.

I would even cry sometimes at my desk about the things I was witnessing in the lives of people who were striving to live for God. It was like a nagging in my soul that wouldn't let me rest.

I had my moment of truth one day, after a business meeting. The outcome of that meeting was so distressing that I drove home and I sat on the curb outside my house to try to gather my emotions before going inside. I had complained so frequently about work that I just knew my family was tired of hearing about it.

As I sat on the curb, tears began to roll down my face. The explosion of emotions was finally erupting. I could no longer suppress the sorrow and disappointment I had felt to witness the acts of what I thought were righteous men and women whose job it was to care for the least of these. I cried out to God that day in frustration and said, "how long, Father? How long must I endure this?."

I felt like I was being punished at the time. Maybe I wasn't supposed to take that job after all. Maybe I should have listened to my husband's suggestion to find something else. God's plan wasn't panning out the way I envisioned it would. This work was painful. This work was exhausting. This work was discouraging at times. But how could this be? I am working in the house of the Lord with others who love the Lord. As I sat on that curb, complaining about how long

I had to endure this punishment, I realized something that arrested my tears for a moment. I realized that I was only experiencing a micro-portion of what God experiences every day when I chose to do what I want to do, instead of what was right.

Every time I choose to not walk in my purpose, someone misses out on the gift that they need from me. Just like the people who needed the help and services of that church missed out, every time they chose to only serve people who they chose to serve.

I had been withholding my gifts from the Kingdom, just like those leaders. I was selectively serving those I was comfortable serving, just like that church.

Personal Reflections

Lesson # 8 The Call is Never Convenient

"Don't make the mistake of believing that your call to purpose will be something that is convenient to your current position."

Who knew that a single act of obedience in a moment of blind faith would lead to such a drastic shift in my life. Actually, there were several small steps of faith the led up to me leaving the workforce to build the ministry full-time. As comfortable as it was to continue collecting a check to do work that I loved, it wasn't enough to keep my spirit at rest.

I knew that God was calling me to something more than just building someone else's vision behind the scenes. He was calling me to actively participate as a leader in building His kingdom. He was calling me out of the traditions of church and the service world of nonprofit to build the lives of people in a more direct and kingdom-focused way.

What did that mean? How was I supposed to do this? Who was supposed to help me? Why me, God?

The day God confirmed in my spirit that I was to leave my salaried job and start the ministry, I was nervous. I had to go home and announce to my new husband that God was calling me to leave my job to start a ministry.

We had been married less than 5 years and we were a blended family, which wasn't blending so well at the time. We had a grandchild living with us, child support, debt, and a big new house and plenty of bills to go with it.

I just knew my husband was going to draw the line and give me an ultimatum. I questioned the logic of it as well.

One of the first sayings I ever adopted from my husband was, "never make for sure bills with maybe money."

He had done a great job of living within his means before this lofty dream chick entered his world. Now suddenly, there's double the kids, double the debt, a house three times the size of his comfy cozy apartment and this short, sassy risk-taking wife who was always talking into doing things outside of his comfort zone. But what was I supposed to do? God said, "GO!." To make matters more complex, I had just changed jobs for an increase a year before.

I spent a couple of months working up the nerve to have the conversation with Erick about what I needed to do. Looking back, I believe he saw the signs of something coming. I was deeply focused on the design of the ministry for weeks before I finally talked to Erick. I know for certain that I am married to a man who knew then and knows now how to trust God.

When I finally mustered the courage to tell him what God was calling me to do, all he said was "okay." Okay! Okay!... I had been rehearsing my speech in order to plead my case. I had prepared a plan to give him for how I was going to make sure I could still carry my weight financially.

It was a quick and simple discussion, too simple for my nervous mind to accept. Even after we had the talk, I kept waiting for him to come back to me and suggest that I wait until a time that would be better for us. But he never did. He simply believed in me and trusted God.

I am a firm believer that God honored Erick's faithfulness, as much as He did my own as Kingdom Communities of the Valley was being launched. I say this because of two specific things that happened immediately after I resigned.

To the people watching, it appeared to some that I was nuts. We had 6 children and one grandchild at the time. However, inwardly, I was sure that I had been called to take this step.

God confirmed it for me by having my former employer be the first to make a $1,000 donation to the ministry, before we had even officially launched. Secondly, he provided me with a contract that paid me very generously for several months, simply for the use of my name. That's right! All I had to do was consent to the use of my name for a project that was being launched within the community where God had called me to serve.

Now, prior to this experience, I felt confident that my reputation was decent. But I never imagined that it was so valuable that an entity would pay me for being associated with it. Needless to say, God was trying to teach me that my value wasn't based on man's perception, but rather His favor was opening doors that I never even dreamed existed.

Personal Reflections

56

57

Lesson # 9 Integrity Matters

Over the course of my professional career, I have been blessed to rise from low-level administrative positions to management positions then ultimately to executive leadership. In some of these positions, I even had the opportunity to lead and manage individuals who held many academic degrees, including doctorates in education and other fields.

No matter what position I held, the one consistent character trait I always observed was pride. Very early on in my professional career, my distaste for what I have witnessed among other leaders cost me to drive to remain as humble as possible with leading other people.

I have worked for leaders who felt comfortable enough in there authority to refer to Black clients and patients as "niggers" in my presence. I have worked with several others who had what I call the "those people "mentality, meaning the people that they perceived to be beneath their stature.

In the midst of situations were despair your flaw would rear its ugly head, sometimes I would remain silent. Other times I would be bold enough to speak up and to speak out about the offensive nature of comments that were made. I was always just careful enough to speak in such a way that did not offend the person who had offended me, until recently.

The last 10 years of my life have been what I considered Boot Camp or training ground for the leader that God has called me to be. I had endured verbal abuse, bullying and clear discrimination on many occasions.

No matter the obstacle, I was blessed by God to be able to persevere through the afflictions and come out of the battle on the other side with all my skin, hair, and teeth intact.

I even managed to not go to jail on several occasions that probably would have provoked such an outcome for me in the past. I didn't recognize it during the years of what I call myself fridge, but God was preparing me for something that I could not handle at the time. But it his appointed time, I was catapulted into greatness. What I thought was the end was actually the beginning of a very marvelous journey to better health better relationships and even financial prosperity.

The ministry God had given me, Kingdom Communities, had reached its third year of operations and I have not produced a full-time salary through my effort to grow the organization. I was feeling pretty discouraged and even question whether God had actually called me to do this work.

I remember bargaining with my husband when I resigned from my job. I explained that within three years I would replace the income that I was leaving behind. I was confident that God would do it. What I didn't realize that God had given me the strength, courage, and wisdom to do it but I was really still afraid of the task.

Being afraid, I spent time building the kingdom under the guise of building the capacity of every other organization around me that was doing good work. Over the course of three years there were so many other ministries and businesses that were launched with my support that I was unable to measure the impact of my gifts.

It was an awesome feeling to look around me and see all of the great work being done and know that I had taken part in the growth and development of each of the ministries and organizations that were changing the lives of people and many other communities. Some pretty awesome things have taken place over the three-year period that were certainly noteworthy for the kingdom.

Unfortunately, although it was very convenient, it was not what God had instructed me to do.

After some reflection, I felt a great deal of disappointment and a sense of failure. I wanted to please God, but I didn't feel like I was equipped to do the job. My alternative was to find a position where I could be the best service and I could be to another Christian leader and organization.

As the ministry introduce fourth year, I had entered the job market to search for a full-time position working for someone else. I needed a reprieve from what I felt was a failed attempt to build something for God's glory. Within three weeks I had two small contracts. Within three months, I have a full-time position that have been created for me within a very reputable Christian organization.

I was so excited. Full-time job with benefits. A decent salary that afforded me the opportunity to begin helping my husband maintain our household on a more consistent basis. Surrounded by brothers and sisters in Christ who were all eager to build the kingdom just like me.

Not!

I entered into a new position only to learn of the quiet chaos that have been brewing within an organization because of new leadership colliding with old traditions and a lot of hidden agendas among my peers.

With my spiritual eyes I recognize the need for prayer and fasting as a part of my daily routine. On a regular basis I would observe opportunities for growth within our organization and I would feed these ideas to my leadership as suggestions for process improvement and program enhancements.

For the first seven months, my enthusiasm and initiative were well received by my leadership.

I even earned the nickname "GetrDone Gal." My boss said he appreciated my ability to identify a problem, create a solution and then get the job done. Sadly, I have garnered so much attention from the leadership that it alienated me from many of my colleagues. And my disillusioned view that we were all working to be excellent and build the kingdom, I continued to be prayerful without being more strategic.

In hindsight, I still would not change a thing about how things transpired because God's plan is so much bigger than any strategy I could ever create.

As appreciative as my boss had been, there came a time during my employ where he was ultimately confronted by other staff and told that I was his favorite pick and that I received special treatment because of it. Because I was privy to most of the chaos that was being addressed by our leadership, I understood his willingness to allow me to be his GetrDone Gal.

My philosophy was that we worked better together within the organization and division would only slow down our progress, so I made every attempt to calm the concerns of my colleagues.

Within 30 days of my boss being confronted about his favoritism, I was fired. Yes, fired. For the first time in my life, I have been terminated from a position. How could this have happened to me? I was the faithful employee who defended him when people talked about his incompetence and his lack of sensitivity.

I was the employee who never whined about being harassed or targeted by my coworkers who were plotting my demise because of my rapid promotion within the organization. I was accused by co-workers of abusing my power after a subordinate wrote a favorable letter for someone close to me.

Although I had no knowledge of the letter, it was suggested that I bullied this person into writing the letter.

When I refused to accept the blame for this employee's actions, I was told that my services were no longer needed. I learned a year or so later that the same employee had been promoted to the position I once held. The organization was paying him nearly $20,000 a year less.

Throughout the ordeal, God kept saying to me "do not compromise my integrity." I would see this message everywhere. I had a choice to make. I could keep my job if I admitted to a lie, or I could lose my job for standing in the unpopular truth. I chose to maintain my integrity.

This experience was both a humbling and sobering reality check. The humility came through understanding that being an over-achiever did not make me immune to termination. The sobering came through understanding that sometimes even the people who put you in position, value their position more than they do righteousness. The right thing to do is not always what people in leadership will choose.

Personal Reflections

Lesson # 10 Not Everyone Will Celebrate With You

"Some of the people you have been serving with your gifts with despise you for choosing to focus on building your own dream instead of theirs"

Personal Reflections